Original title:
The House Beneath the Stars

Copyright © 2025 Creative Arts Management OÜ
All rights reserved.

Author: Isabella Rosemont
ISBN HARDBACK: 978-1-80587-096-8
ISBN PAPERBACK: 978-1-80587-566-6

A Tapestry of Stellar Tales

In the backyard, a chair swings,
With a dog that barks at moonlit things.
The cat just yawns, an unimpressed sight,
While fireflies dance in the cool of night.

Up above, the stars start to giggle,
As comets zoom in a cosmic wiggle.
A squirrel's lost his acorn up high,
While planets spin round like they're in a pie.

Grandpa claims he's a starry sage,
Spinning tales from another age.
He says the Milky Way is just spilled milk,
And that the sun wears a dress of silk.

But just last week, with a wink and a grin,
He thought a shooting star was just a gin.
Oh, the laughter that erupts from the ground,
As nighttime whispers secrets all around.

Echoes of Starlight in the Stillness

In the garden at midnight, crickets play,
While I search for my shoes that ran away.
The cat's on the roof, practicing flight,
Dreaming of cheese in the pale moonlight.

The shadows they wiggle, dance with glee,
As squirrels tease me from the old oak tree.
I offer a snack, they just laugh and scamper,
While I chase my thoughts like a restless pamper.

A Home Cradled by Constellations

With a telescope aimed at an old wooden fence,
I tried to count stars, it made no sense.
The dog thinks it's playtime, barks at the sky,
While I fumble for notes in my pocket nearby.

The neighbor's voice echoes, his old tunes ring,
As I tap my foot, feeling like a king.
But a raccoon appears, my snack thief tonight,
We strike a deal, he won't start a fight.

Twilight Murmurs

Under twinkling lights on a cool summer eve,
I wrestle with shadows, I can hardly believe.
The fireflies stumble, like tipsy old men,
While my jokes float away, lost in the zen.

The moon winks brightly, a mischievous sprite,
As I discover a marshmallow fight mid-bite.
My friends laugh and giggle, the night feels so free,
In this cosmic circus, we're all family.

Beneath the Infinite Canopy

The stars are actors on a stage up high,
While I bow to the moon, my esteemed ally.
The backyard's a kingdom, the branches my throne,
With a crown made of daisies, I feel like a loan.

Laughter erupts as the clouds roll away,
We hide from the owls who come out to play.
Each moment is silly, a comic delight,
Beneath this vast canvas, all feels just right.

Stellar Dreams Unfold

In pajamas that twinkle bright,
We dance with comets in the night.
Our bed's a spaceship, off we soar,
To slumber parties on Jupiter's floor.

Galactic giggles fill the air,
As aliens burst in everywhere!
We tell them jokes, they laugh with glee,
While floating past the old Moon's tree.

Shooting stars drop ice cream cones,
We munch on laughter and cosmic tones.
Underneath the Milky Way's grin,
We drift in dreams where fun begins.

The Family of the Milky Way

Dad roams space with his silly hat,
Mom's in orbit, chasing after a cat.
Sister's painting planets in rainbow hues,
While brother's got his moonwalking shoes.

Toasts of stardust, we cheer and play,
In our spaceship, every day's a holiday.
We're the quirky crew of a cosmic fleet,
With asteroid snacks and meteorite treats.

Dance parties on Saturn's rings,
Our family tree is full of quirky things.
We share our tales with stars as our friends,
In the galaxy where fun never ends.

A Nest of Nighttime Stories

Underneath the glowing skies,
We gather 'round with bright, wide eyes.
Tales of planets and their quirks,
Like Martians who can't do their homework.

The moon's a lamp for my cat to chase,
While stars play tag in outer space.
We giggle at meteors racing by,
And dream of space pies that never die.

In a cozy nest, stories unfold,
Of brave astronauts and treasures of gold.
With laughter stitched into every seam,
We drift away in a cozy dream.

Cosmic Corners of Comfort

In our nook and cozy chair,
We find constellations hiding there.
With snacks of stardust and fizzy drinks,
We ponder what a black hole thinks.

Silly stories, we share out loud,
While asteroids bounce, drawing a crowd.
The couch transforms to a rocket ride,
As laughter echoes through the cosmic tide.

In our corner, the universe is small,
Where fun and comfort always call.
With cuddly pillows and stars to guide,
We explore galactic joy, side by side.

Through the Window of a Cosmic Heart

I peek through glass, what do I see?
A cat on a rocket, sipping iced tea.
The moon winks at me, with a grin so wide,
And comets play tag on a celestial slide.

Each star's a lightbulb, flickering bright,
A dance party's brewing, oh what a sight!
Asteroids throwing confetti in dash,
While aliens are jiving, oh ain't it a blast?

Soft Radiance from Distant Suns

In this cosmic cafe, we serve stardust lattes,
With cosmic cookies and those supernova pastries.
A giant starfish sings while sitting in space,
Twirling round planets with an elegant grace.

The laughter of meteors rings out so clear,
As space squirrels giggle, drinking space beer.
What fun in the void, nothing's quite bizarre,
When you're slow dancing with a flying guitar!

The Lullaby of Twinkling Light

Little sparkles sing, oh what a tune,
In pajamas of starlight they groove 'til the moon.
A polar bear spinning with a lime green kite,
Sleeps while dreaming of a pancake delight.

Galactic giggles float on cosmic breeze,
While every planet shakes its fuzzy knees.
A rocket crew snoozes, wrapped in soft hugs,
With their dreams all tangled in space fuzzy rugs.

Tales Crafted by the Nebulae

Nebulae whisper, spinning wild tales,
Of disco ball planets and glittery sails.
A zebra-shaped spaceship sails through the night,
While space-fairies dance, their dresses so bright.

Count the lightyears, they tumble and spin,
Each puff of dust brings a chuckle and grin.
With humor so stellar, their laughter will rise,
In a quilt of stardust, under twinkling skies.

Crickets Sing Under Cosmic Light

Crickets chirp in the twilight,
While moths dance in delight.
They twirl with starry grace,
In an interstellar race.

A raccoon joins the fun,
Wearing shades, he's number one.
He sips his cosmic drink,
While we all just stop and think.

The frogs croak a silly tune,
Underneath the glowing moon.
They serenade the space bees,
Who swoosh by with cosmic ease.

Laughter echoes through the night,
As bugs clash in a dance fight.
Stars giggle at the scene,
In this galactic routine.

Sheltered Beneath Infinite Dreams

A turtle snoozes on a mat,
Beside a space-time acrobat.
The clock ticks, but who's keeping score?
When dreams of jellybeans galore!

The walls are painted bright and wild,
With alien colors, like a child.
Monsters nap in comfy chairs,
Wearing socks with silly flares.

A hamster writes a cosmic tale,
About a cat who rode a whale.
Each chapter ends with a loud roar,
And readers shout, "We need more!"

This shelter of whimsical delight,
Turns each moment into a flight.
Where funny dreams and visions play,
Each evening ends in a ballet.

In the Arms of Astral Whispers

Squirrels gossip in the sky,
With twinkling stars swimming by.
They trade jokes of cosmic bounds,
While laughter spins in dizzy rounds.

A wise old owl tells tales galore,
Of a cat who thought he'd soar.
He puffed up like a balloon,
But forgot the check for the moon!

A playful breeze strokes the trees,
Tickling branches with such ease.
They giggle and sway in delight,
Under the canopy of night.

In the arms of cosmic schemes,
We wake up lost in funny dreams.
With tales of laughter and grace,
We find magic in each place.

Stardust Over the Hearth

The fireplace roars with cheer,
As stardust shakes off its fear.
It sparkles, dances, and misbehaves,
While we roast marshmallows like brave knaves.

A couch potato snail joins us,
Patting his shell with much fuss.
He claims he's the king of snacks,
While munching on old pizza packs.

The plants crack jokes with sly roots,
And wear hats made of old boots.
They laugh as the shadows grow wide,
In this cosmic joyride.

Stardust sprinkles from the beams,
Enveloping us in funny dreams.
So gather 'round this merry space,
As laughter lights up every face.

Echoing Moments Beneath the Skies

In a world where shadows dance,
The cat wore a hat, taking a chance.
Whispers of giggles float through the night,
As owls start rapping, a comical sight.

Socks with sandals, a fashion faux pas,
Naps interrupted by an old raccoon's claws.
The stars above wink with delight,
While aliens chuckle, oh what a sight!

With lemonade rivers and cookies galore,
Dance like no one's watching on a starlit floor.
Hiccups and laughter spill from the trees,
As fireflies giggle, carrying the breeze.

So raise a toast to the chaos we find,
In echoing moments that tickle the mind.
With each silly giggle, the night has a glow,
And the moon just chuckles, "Oh, put on a show!"

Where Beliefs Sail on Starlit Winds

Dreamers float on clouds of dreams,
While socks go missing, or so it seems.
Balloons filled with giggles set to explore,
As dreams sail out to the cosmic shore.

Silly ideas on a moonbeam glide,
Like a cat wearing goggles, oh what a ride!
With mischief mapped out in the night's embrace,
The stars erupt in a twinkling race.

Kites made of wishes, chasing the breeze,
Finding lost spoons with relative ease.
A unicorn jokes about potato chips,
As laughter washes over in cosmic sips.

So let's sail where nonsense leads,
Where laughter is plenty and fun never creeds.
Under a quilt of stars, let's boldly tread,
Chasing wild dreams as the sun spins ahead!

Flickering Images in an Astral Realm

Twinkling lights paint a playful scene,
Jellybeans flying by like they're on a screen.
Wizards on hoverboards, a magical sight,
While gravity giggles, defying the night.

Pizza slices drift in the misty air,
As dancing penguins show off their flair.
With each twinkle launching a comet of cheese,
The stars chuckle lightly, as they aim to please.

Whispers of laughter flow like a stream,
With tacos and rhythm, we dance and we dream.
Galactic marbles roll down from the sky,
While cosmic critters pass by with a sigh.

In this realm where the playful convene,
Each flickering image a part of the scene.
So grab your sleighs and let's ride on this beam,
In whimsical wonder, we'll chase every dream!

Beyond the Horizon of Dreams

In a land where rubber chickens reign,
The sun wears sunglasses, oh how insane!
With squirrels who juggle on a trampoline,
And singing rainbows drift through the scene.

Beyond the horizon, where giggles collide,
Where candy corn trees grow tall with pride.
The clouds wear pajamas, all fluffy and bright,
While the stars snicker softly, all through the night.

Jumping over puddles of fizzy delight,
With weird snacks dancing, oh what a sight!
An octopus plays drums made from pie,
As unicorns leap, soaring high in the sky.

We frolic through dreams, with whimsy to spare,
With laughter ablaze, like a warm summer air.
So let's explore all beyond what we scheme,
In this playful world, we're free to dream!

Dwellings Wrapped in Night's Embrace

In a cozy nook where shadows play,
The cat tells secrets at the end of the day.
A mismatch of socks in a cupboard reveal,
The mysteries of how chaos can heal.

Under blankets piled high like a mountain,
Cocoa spills over, a warm, sweet fountain.
We dance in our pajamas, quite the sight,
With disco moves that shine in the night.

Whispers of laughter sneak out through the pane,
The neighbor's dog joins in, barking our refrain.
With star-shaped cookies, we feast like kings,
In this night-time castle, oh, the joy it brings!

So here's to the ramblings, the giggles and sighs,
Our dreams float around like the strange fireflies.
In this wondrous abode of quirk and delight,
We weave our adventures 'neath the soft starlight.

Stargazer's Refuge

Where pillows are planets and dreams take flight,
We map out the skies, with giggles and light.
The telescope's aimed at the wrong end, oh dear,
What's that? Is it Mars, or just grandma's beer?

Beneath a glow-in-the-dark, stick-on moon,
We conjure wild tales, we'll finish real soon.
The blanket fort kingdom is strong and well-built,
With fortifications of leftover quilt.

Our laughter rings out like a chorus of glee,
With snacks that are questionable, still tasty, we see.
The starry-night fears our sugary might,
As we conquer the universe, one candy at a bite.

In this crazy haven, no rules apply,
A sprinkle of wonder, a dollop of why.
With whimsy our guide, we soar and we crash,
In this refuge of joy, where dreams make a splash!

Memoirs of the Moonlit Retreat

In a cozy garage, our kingdom resides,
With treasures from childhood, each one, a guide.
Garage-sale gems that we claim as our own,
Turn ordinary nights into legends well-known.

With twinkling lights that hang on the wall,
We fashion a disco and we have a ball.
The dog in a tutu proudly parades,
As we spin and twirl, in our moonlit charades.

Each snack contains magic, a dash of delight,
A mishmash of goodies under soft, starry light.
With soda explosions that boost our delight,
Our memoirs are written in laughter tonight.

So we raise our glasses, filled high with sweet cheer,
To nights spent in joy, for we've no room for fear.
With hearts ever open, we dream big and bold,
In this moonlit retreat, countless stories unfold!

Serendipity Under Infinite Skies

Under cosmic wonder where dreams intertwine,
We stumble on laughter in moments divine.
A flying pizza slice? We swear that we saw,
Or was it the cat who decided to claw?

With shadows that wiggle and giggle around,
Secret laughter echoes, it's silly and sound.
Exploring the madness of socks without mates,
We fashion a life that celebrates fates.

The dance of the comets is best done in pairs,
As we trip over stardust and tumble down stairs.
Our blank-paper rockets soar high up above,
While we ponder the mysteries of watermelon love.

A sprinkle of chaos, sparkles of fun,
In this great universe, we're never outdone.
With the moon as our witness, the stars as our guides,
We write our own stories, nowhere to hide.

The Cottage of Astral Tales

In a cottage snug and bright,
Where dust bunnies take their flight,
A raccoon in a chair reclines,
Reading ancient cosmic signs.

The cats engage in deep debates,
Of cheese and mice and other fates,
While shadows dance upon the floor,
Valuable secrets, we can't ignore.

Beneath the roof, with laughter's flare,
Silly stories fill the air,
A telescope that sees the past,
Uh-oh! The moon has lost its cast!

So come inside, the fun awaits,
With cosmic pies and starry plates,
Where giggles spark like shooting stars,
And dreams are cooked in glass jars.

Lanterns in the Galactic Glow

A lantern swings with swagger bold,
And winks at tales of knights of old,
While shadows sidestep with a grin,
This party is where fun begins!

With interstellar snacks on trays,
Like popcorn moons and comet pays,
Space fruit floats, a curious sight,
Bananas with a twinkly bite.

Aliens with party hats appear,
Doing the cha-cha with a cheer,
They break-dance on the living room floor,
Carrying secrets of the galore!

So gather 'round, let laughter spread,
With cosmic tunes, we'll dance instead,
For in this glow of endless nights,
We laugh beneath our starlit lights.

Nights of Wonder: A Celestial Escape

Under a blanket of cosmic glee,
We snack on stardust—just you and me,
With martians playing cards in the corner,
This night gets funnier and a bit warmer!

A comet whizzes past our door,
Convinced it's here to start a war,
But wait! It missed, now it's a bee,
Buzzing by, just look and see.

Silly owls in velvet gowns,
Composing tunes of far-off towns,
While shooting stars, in groups of three,
Debate who's the best at hide and see!

So let the night unfold with glee,
With quirky tales of galaxy spree,
For every twinkle hides a grin,
In our celestial realm, we win!

Twilight's Embrace in the Quiet Nook

As twilight dips its brush in ink,
The fireflies gather—what do you think?
With lanterns hung on every branch,
The squirrels dance, creating their chance!

The owl hosts trivia, all in jest,
As turtles play cards, they feel the best,
With pudding made of moonlit cream,
It's the oddest party you could dream!

Each tick of the clock is met with cheer,
As stars chuckle down, drawing near,
The cosmos love a playful jest,
In this nook, we are truly blessed!

So come on in, don't be so shy,
Join in the fun, let out a sigh,
For laughter echoes through the night,
In our cosmic cozy delight!

Ghostly Whispers of Light

When night falls soft and deep,
A ghostly cat takes a leap.
With shadows laughing in their play,
They dance around and drift away.

The toaster pops with quite a grin,
As friendly ghosts invite us in.
They share their tales of ancient glee,
While sipping tea in jubilee.

A Sanctuary Amidst the Cosmos

In a cozy nook where giggles soar,
The aliens knock at the kitchen door.
They bring green snacks and silly hats,
And laugh with us over raucous chats.

With floating chairs and stars so bright,
They dance like silly fools all night.
Our laughter echoes through the space,
As we twirl and spin in endless grace.

Celestial Lanterns of Hope

The light bulbs wink with cosmic cheer,
They flicker secrets for all to hear.
With each soft glow, a mischievous tease,
As they whistle tunes that sway the breeze.

A comet's tail spills jolly light,
Turning chores into pure delight.
We hop and cheer, with hearts so bold,
While telling stories, never old.

A Universe Wrapped in Warmth

Beneath a quilt of fluffy dreams,
A universe bursts at the seams.
With cookies baking, spirits rise,
As we share giggles 'neath candy skies.

Each star a cookie, sweet and round,
Our laughter echoed all around.
We pull the blankets, snug and tight,
In this cozy realm of pure delight.

Secrets of the Nocturnal Dwelling

In the attic, the raccoons play,
Throwing moon pies on their holiday.
While owls wear spectacles to read,
The gossip of the night's great deed.

The shadows dance with a quirky tune,
Mice in top hats twirl under the moon.
A cat is judging this grand charade,
With a smirk that's perfectly displayed.

Light flickers from a neon sign,
Saying 'Welcome! This night is divine!'
Fireflies sparkle in a graceful row,
Balloons float high with a cheeky glow.

Waking neighbors with laughter's cheer,
As crickets chime in, lending an ear.
The night air whispers tales so bright,
In this whimsical, starry delight.

A Sanctuary Among the Constellations

Beneath the vast, absurd terrain,
Frogs croak lyrics to a silly strain.
Fireflies dance in their fancy shoes,
While raccoons critique the latest news.

Stars giggle from their heavenly stroll,
As a hedgehog claims a role in a scroll.
A picnic's laid with pies and jests,
All night long, we count our guests.

The pumpkins gossip with soft, round grins,
As beetles hum their jazzy spins.
Under the arch of twinkling lights,
Each wink from above ignites our nights.

With blankets spread and dreams unfurled,
Laughter echoes across the world.
In this silly sanctuary's embrace,
Even the moon has a chuckling face.

Reflections on Midnight's Porch

On the porch, the night unfolds,
With secrets shared and stories bold.
A squirrel spills coffee, what a feat,
While crickets tap their tiny feet.

The rocking chair creaks with delight,
As the raccoons sing 'Let's dance all night!'
Each shadow sways, a partner, true,
With a goofy grin, they join the crew.

Stars peek down with a twinkly wink,
As owls give toast and stop to think.
The teapot whistles, but it's not outdone,
By the chattering gang having their fun.

The porch light hums a merry song,
As laughter flows, it can't go wrong.
Midnight chatter, sweet and spry,
While moonbeams dance from way up high.

The Abode of Celestial Gleams

Here in this realm of glitter and cheer,
Squirrels in pajamas toast with beers.
The stars are tickled by laughing trees,
And the wind blows giggles with the breeze.

A hedgehog brings pies, such a spread,
While moonlight paints all that's said.
The porch become a carnival stage,
Where laughter thrives and sage turns page.

Cards are shuffled, night games unfold,
With playful banter and antics bold.
The winks of stars keep spirits alive,
As frogs in tuxedos take a dive.

Jokes and riddles liven the night,
With each twin star, a new delight.
In this celestial abode, we play,
Counting laughs 'til the break of day.

Under a Canopy of Light

Under the twinkling dots so bright,
We set up camp, oh what a sight!
A raccoon stole our pizza pie,
While owls laughed as they floated by.

We tried to count each shining star,
But lost count near the candy jar.
The frogs croaked jokes, so loud and clear,
While the crickets played a symphony near.

The fireflies joined, with flickering glee,
Dancing around, as wild as can be.
"Just don't trip," we laughed, all aglow,
As we stumbled through the forest below.

So let's toast marshmallows, oh what fun,
Under the smile of a big, bright sun.
And when the night's laughter starts to bloom,
We'll find silly shapes in the evening's gloom.

Whispers of the Night Sky

Beneath the whispers of night's embrace,
We spotted shapes that made us laugh with grace.
A cow, a cloud, a floating shoe,
Who knew the cosmos had such a view?

Aliens peeked from circles bold,
Claiming our snacks, oh if truth be told!
They left us some chips, it's true they snuck,
Yet laughed so hard, we ran amok.

As we made wishes on falling stars,
We swore we heard the moon playing guitars.
With giggles high, we danced in delight,
Under the giggles of the whimsical night.

The owls hooted, "You're all a bunch of fools!"
As we sat together, our merry little drool.
With hearts so light, and skies so wide,
We found our joy, and tucked it inside.

Sanctuary of Celestial Wonders

In a realm where laughter meets the sky,
We chuckled as satellites whizzed by.
A comet tripped, and oh how it fell,
Leaving stardust trails, a sparkly spell.

The constellations played cards at night,
"Go fish!" they shouted, in radiant light.
We drew in a circle, wrapped tight with dreams,
While the Milky Way shared its forgotten memes.

Twirling planets pranked the sleeping sun,
"Catch us if you can!" they shouted in fun.
We joined the jokes in the cosmic dance,
With dreams so silly, we'd take a chance.

So grab a friend and share a smile,
As stars giggle, let's stay awhile.
In this sanctuary of cosmic cheer,
Funny tales echo, all night near.

Where Shadows Dance with Moonbeams

In a world where shadows flip and sway,
Moonbeams join in the nighttime play.
The bushes laugh, the trees all cheer,
As we dance around with no sense of fear.

Jokes tumble out like leaves in fall,
And the night air carries them to all.
We played pretend as ghosts with flair,
In the glow of the moon, we didn't care.

Whispers tickle from the breeze so light,
As we chased our dreams into the night.
Each twinkling glow sang a silly tune,
As we pranced together, beneath the moon.

So if you find a shadow that seems quite bright,
It's just us laughing, under starlit might.
Join us in silliness, come take the chance,
Where shadows dance, in a merry, moonlit trance.

Moonflower Dreams Unravel

Under a moon that giggles bright,
Dreamers dance in silver light.
They wear hats made of cheese and toast,
Chasing shadows, what a boast!

Jellybeans rain from above,
As ducklings sing of silly love.
With cupcakes spinning in the breeze,
They twirl around like clumsy fleas.

In gardens where the fairies play,
A hedgehog hosts a wild ballet.
With twinkling eyes and squeaky shoes,
They stomp and hop, who could refuse?

As laughter floats on dandelion fluff,
There's no such thing as just enough.
In moonflower dreams, the night is bold,
A circus of stories waiting to be told.

Celestial Journeys from Within

All aboard the cosmic train,
Where unicorns dance in the rain.
Galactic snacks, a feast divine,
With milkshake stars that brightly shine.

Space cats sing opera on the moon,
While asteroids tap a funny tune.
Stargazers giggle as they float,
On a bubblegum-flavored boat.

The comets race, but who's the champ?
A turtle wearing a glow-in-dark lamp!
With cosmic moss growing in their hair,
They play hopscotch with the solar flare.

So laugh out loud, embrace the fun,
The universe has just begun.
Adventures lie in twists and bends,
In laughter where every journey ends.

Mysteries of the Velvet Sky

In the velvet sky, a tale unfolds,
Of singing squirrels with secrets untold.
They whisper riddles to the stars,
While juggling planets, wishing on cars.

A sandwich flies on a comet's tail,
While moonbeams giggle at the tale.
With flapping wings, a turtle glides,
Over marshmallow clouds, he slides.

Chasing meteors made of candy,
Oh, what a cosmic sort of dandy!
Galaxies twist in a joyful waltz,
As planets gather, with no faults.

So if you gaze at the twinkling night,
Know that fun wraps the universe tight.
In velvet whispers, let the laughter play,
As mysteries dance and frolic away.

Stardust Memories Echo

In a realm where giggles twirl,
And stardust wraps around the whirl,
The memories echo, loud and cheery,
Of hopping cats who feel quite fairy.

With rainbow fish that ride the clouds,
And bouncing bunnies, oh so proud.
They paint the sky in colors bright,
With silly hats that cause delight.

The echoes shimmer, stories leap,
While sleepy stars begin to peep.
Each twinkling tale is a laugh parade,
In a universe lovingly made.

So cherish these echoes of fun and cheer,
In every heartbeat that you hear.
For stardust dreams weave quirky threads,
Of joy and laughter, where no one dreads.

Whispers of Celestial Shadows

In a garden where gnomes dance,
Under the moon, they take a stance.
They whisper secrets, loud and clear,
About lost socks and the last beer.

Fish fly by with a twinkling eye,
Chasing thoughts that drift and sigh.
The crickets don a tiny hat,
Debating loudly where the cheese is at.

Stars hold a giggle, quite absurd,
As comets chase the singing bird.
Laughter echoes through the night,
While squirrels plot their next big flight.

Fairies play cards with the sky's great glow,
Betting on dreams, putting on a show.
Then they vanish, a sudden spray,
Leaving behind a joke or two to play.

When Dreams Meet the Night Sky

A pillow fight with the fluffy clouds,
While dreams dance free in giggling crowds.
Shooting stars slide past with flair,
Stealing secrets from the night air.

A comet's tail sparkles like cheese,
Making wishes that aim to please.
Up above, the owls tell jokes,
While hiding from some playful folks.

The moon's full, a giant pie,
As dreams float up and wave goodbye.
A kite takes flight on a shooting breeze,
And lands with grace among the trees.

In the dark, the shadows prance,
Making merry with a silly dance.
Underneath a wink of moonlight,
Everything feels just perfectly right.

Beneath the Cosmic Canopy

Under twinkling lights we play,
A game of tag in cosmic sway.
Galaxies swirl with a lively spin,
As laughter echoes, our nightly din.

Asteroids tumble, a rockstar show,
Dancing fast, putting on a glow.
The meteors sip on stardust tea,
And share old tales of cosmic glee.

A bright star stubs its tiny toe,
What a sight, the dance of woe!
But soon it grins, with a laugh did say,
"I'll shine brighter in a comical way!"

Each wink and twirl from afar,
Spells a joy, our guiding star.
In this playground of endless night,
We find our dreams in pure delight.

Echoes in the Starlit Haven

In this haven where the shadows play,
Silly creatures sing songs of clay.
Napping bears wear party hats,
While raccoons plot with lots of chatter.

A moonbeam pops a balloon with glee,
As space ducks waddle, full of spree.
The owls are wise, but oh so sly,
They burst into fits, and laugh, oh my!

Constellations fidget in the breeze,
Taking turns to crack up and tease.
Planetary pranks fill the air,
As stars spin stories without a care.

Echoes of laughter mingle and glide,
Through the night where whimsy can't hide.
In this starlit realm, nothing seems grim,
Just endless joy on the cosmic whim.

Wonderment in Celestial Corners

In a room where giggles roam,
The ceiling's a cosmic dome.
With socks that dance on the floor,
And shadows that peek at the door.

A cat stares at the bright moon,
Thinking it's a giant balloon.
Chasing dust bunnies up high,
Dreaming of treats from the sky.

Laughter echoes in the night,
As we take off on silly flight.
With chairs turned into rocket ships,
And snacks packed for cosmic trips.

In corners where wonder blooms,
We find adventure in our rooms.
A place where joy never ends,
With silly stars as our friends.

Journeys Through Twilight's Threshold

When night falls on our humble shack,
We wear pajamas, not a lack.
With flashlights bright we start to roam,
In search of snacks and cosmic foam.

The fridge becomes a starry sea,
Exploring flavors wild and free.
A sandwich sails on a plate,
As we navigate our fate.

Around us twinkling bright,
Are thoughts of giggles in the night.
With cookies as our guiding light,
We conquer the kitchen's height.

A journey through the evening's glow,
Where the only limit's our own show.
With laughter ringing loud and clear,
We embrace the joy that's always near.

Celestial Abode

In our dwelling where dreams collide,
Every shadow has a playful side.
The curtains wave like sails in glee,
As we tap-dance to the symphony.

The stars outside might make us sigh,
But here inside, we reach for the sky.
With cushions piled like clouds of fun,
We launch our voyages one by one.

The fridge hums songs of midnight treats,
As we join in with our dancing feet.
With socks that slide and giggles loud,
We make the cosmos feel so proud.

In every crevice, laughter lives,
As bedtime stories take their gives.
With spirits high, the night goes far,
In our cheerful little avatar.

A Rooftop of Dreams

On the roof where wishes play,
We share our secrets night and day.
With stars as our audience bright,
We pitch our tents with pure delight.

A pizza box becomes a stage,
As we unleash our inner sage.
With voices loud and antics grand,
In this laughter-filled wonderland.

The moon winks at our silly tunes,
While we dance beneath the fluffy blooms.
With magic dust from our imaginations,
We conquer worlds without limitations.

Up here, the universe seems near,
With every giggle we hold dear.
On a rooftop of joy and play,
Where dreams and laughter lead the way.

Memory Lane in the Twilight Realm

In a garden of socks, we dance in delight,
Where shadows throw parties, and cats take flight.
With watches that tick, backwards in time,
We laugh as we slip on a rhyme without chime.

Fireflies in bowties measure our wits,
While we juggle our dreams and the weirdest bits.
A trampoline moon bounces high in the air,
As we chase after giggles without a care.

Catch a comet with candy, oh what a treat!
Twinkle-toed fairies tap-dance on our feet.
Every misstep and tumble's met with a cheer,
For the joy of the night is what we hold dear.

So raise up a glass filled with starlight and glee,
To our odd little world, just you wait and see.
In this twilight realm, we frolic and play,
With each silly moment, we dance the night away.

The Night Wraps Us in Dreams

In pajamas of laughter, we drift and we sway,
Concocting wild stories till the break of day.
With pillows as clouds, we float on soft beams,
As the night wraps around us, and laughter redeems.

The moon pulls a prank, sending giggles our way,
While stars wear both capes and their crowns made of hay.
With marshmallow comets brushing past our heads,
We chuckle with glee as we float on our beds.

A midnight parade of odd pets in disguise,
March past in a conga, oh how time flies!
They're all wearing hats made of colorful fluff,
In this dreamy melange, it's never too tough.

Just follow the lanterns that wiggle and glow,
As we share all our secrets, not one of them slow.
In the land of our dreams where fun reigns supreme,
We'll dance till the twilight unravels the scene.

Hearts Floating in Celestial Currents

With strings on our fingers, we flutter like kites,
Our hearts set afloat on these whimsical nights.
Comets parade on banana peels tight,
While we sip on the juice of a starry delight.

The skies play a game, with clouds up for rent,
We giggle at shadows, they're simply content.
An orchestra of chirps and chuckles align,
As we bounce on the breeze, feeling oh-so-divine.

Wishing on wishes that bounce off the walls,
Finding treasure in laughter, beneath the moon's calls.
With dreams as our sails, we float ever free,
A celestial current, just you, and me.

So wink at the night, let your worries unbind,
Let's gather the starlight, leave sanity behind.
In these frolicsome waves, our spirits entwine,
With hearts full of giggles, forever we shine.

Crooning to the Cosmic Breeze

A melody whispers through trees made of light,
As we sing silly songs in the warmth of the night.
Stars clap their hands to our joyful tunes,
While the cosmos itself croons beneath silver moons.

We strum on the air with guitars made of beams,
Chasing quirks of the night with our hilarious dreams.
As the sun takes a nap, we steal its warm glow,
With a wink and a grin, we take center stage show.

Though the moon sometimes yawns, we push right along,

Creating a night where the weird feels so strong.
In this charming embrace of the wind's gentle tease,
We find joy in the notes of our cosmic breeze.

So gather your giggles, let's tiptoe and sway,
As the stars serenade us in their luminous play.
We'll croon to the heavens with humor so bright,
In this whimsical world, everything feels just right.

Secrets of the Starry Dwelling

A cat on the roof, planning a flight,
With dreams of whiskers all through the night.
He swears he'll dance with the crescent moon,
While dodging the broom of the neighbor's loon.

The fridge hums a tune, a snack's in sight,
As leftovers twirl in the fridge's light.
Whispers of chocolate, chips, and some cheese,
All part of the fun, if you know how to tease.

The dog in the yard, barking at Mars,
Wonders if squirrels are made of candy bars.
He thinks he can catch them, a noble quest,
While chasing his tail in a dizzying jest.

Jars filled with secrets, like pickles in brine,
Knowing that laughter makes everything fine.
So raise a toast with a cup full of cheer,
To the silliest dreams that we hold so dear.

Echoing Lullabies from the Cosmos

In a little nook where the raindrops hum,
A sock puppet sings to the beats of a drum.
Beckoning stars with a wink and a smile,
While we giggle quietly, just for a while.

The moon says hello with a wink and a nod,
As fireflies dance to their nightly applaud.
A chorus of crickets providing the tunes,
While we sway to the rhythm with laughter and spoons.

Behind a glass door, the cat's eye does gleam,
Chasing its tail like it's stuck in a dream.
Oh, what a circus beneath roofs so bright,
With laughter that echoes through the stillness of night.

Dreams tumble out like balloons in the dark,
As we chase after wishes, fun's very own spark.
A lullaby whispers, soft, sweet, and low,
As giggles cascade like a soft afterglow.

Moonlit Refuge

In the backyard maze, our fort made of sheets,
Where we tell the best tales and share our sweet treats.
A fort of giggles and moonlight so bright,
Guarded by teddy bears, ready for flight.

A raccoon named Ricky drops by for some fun,
With a wink and a grin, he's always on the run.
He steals all the cookies and dances away,
Leaving us laughing until break of day.

With pillows as pillows and dreams made of fluff,
We conjure up laughter, just never enough.
As the stars play charades, with winks and with twirls,
We wait for a comet to slide by in swirls.

So here's to the nights where the silliness reigns,
Where laughter rejoices and nothing contains.
In a world full of wonder, let your heart see,
How funny it is to just let yourself be.

Beneath the Night's Embrace

On the patio swing, where dreams intertwine,
We invite all the critters, like old friends of mine.
A raccoon named Benny shares stories of cheese,
While ants line up neatly, just begging for peas.

Every star up above is a wink or a laugh,
While we toast with soda, our favorite craft.
With laughter exploding, like firecrackers bright,
We giggle at shadows that dance in the night.

And suddenly, there's a comet's wild flight,
Shooting through the sky, what a marvelous sight!
We cheer and we shout, what a grand little show,
As socks take to flying, mixed up in the flow.

So remember this tale, of joy and of fun,
In a world full of whimsy, there's never just one.
As we bask 'neath the winks of the cosmic embrace,
Let laughter guide souls in this magical space.

Comfort Found in Stellar Glow

In a room where shadows play,
Laughter dances through the day.
Cookies crumble, crumbs take flight,
As cats plot mischief into the night.

Teapots whistle, jugs do spill,
While socks escape with joyous thrill.
Beneath the light, we brush our fears,
And find surprise in floating beers.

Stars peek in through curtain seams,
Their twinkling spark inspires our dreams.
Each snicker, giggle fills the space,
As we toast with cups we can't replace.

So gather close beneath the beams,
In this cozy world of glowing schemes.
With every burst of joy and cheer,
We find our comfort, year after year.

A Realm Where Light Kept Watch

In a corner where the ripples shine,
We share our snacks, you bring the wine.
The toaster's croon, a silly beat,
Our dance-off starts with shuffling feet.

Pillow fights and outrageous dreams,
We giggle at our childhood themes.
The light bulb winks, it knows our fate,
As we plot our pranks and celebrate.

Underneath this laughter-packed dome,
The air is thick with fun, our home.
Every shadow hides a punchline,
As we toast again to waste our time.

With bubbles floating in the air,
We concoct schemes without a care.
This realm of joy, where light kept watch,
Holds echoes of laughter, no need to botch.

Under the Vastness of Eternity

In a space where silliness reigns,
We gather thoughts like runaway trains.
Jokes bubble up like fizzy soda,
While the clock blinks 'please, come, slow down!'

Blankets piled high, a fortress grand,
Where the remote plays in our hands.
Pizza boxes stacked like the heavens,
On this starry night, we learn our lessons.

With whispered secrets and goofy grins,
We stumble and trip as the fun begins.
Each munch and crunch fills our souls,
Under this vastness, joy's the goal.

So let's be silly, no time for fright,
In this cosmic dance, everything's light.
With each fleeting moment, we shall delight,
Under the vastness, our hearts take flight.

Where the Universe Tells Tales

In a nook where giggles swirl,
We spin wild stories, let 'em unfurl.
The cat yawns, the dog just snores,
As we recreate epic folklore.

The fridge hums a joyful tune,
While midnight snacks are our monsoon.
With cereal hats and cocoa cups,
We crown our victories in clinking clups.

Whispers of stars in every nook,
In search of gold from the storybook.
We craft our realm with giggling glee,
Where the universe listens, just you and me.

Let's spin these tales, oh so divine,
With every laugh, our spirits align.
So come join in, don't take the fall,
In this wild world, there's room for all.

Celestial Connections Gather Here

In a cozy nook up high,
Aliens dance, oh my!
With laughter echoing wide,
They munch on cosmic pie.

Martians play a funky tune,
While comets glide past the moon.
Jovial shouts fill the air,
In the galactic fair with flair.

UFOs serve drinks with zest,
As shooting stars can't take a rest.
The Milky Way spins in glee,
A space party, come and see!

With stardust sprinkled about,
Who knew space could be so sprout?
Connections made with a wink,
Intergalactic fun, don't blink!

Reflections of the Celestial Waters

In a puddle reflecting the sky,
Frogs boast about the stars up high.
They wear tiny hats, oh so bright,
Claiming to leap to cosmic height.

The fish argue who swims the best,
With dreams of space as their quest.
They splash around, causing a scene,
While ducklings quack in between.

Crickets serenade the night,
Singing tunes that feel just right.
In the reflections, laughter's found,
Joyous ripples all around!

With a wink from the moon's soft glow,
Each creature puts on a show.
In this watery verse of fun,
The universe feels like one!

A Whispering Cradle of the Milky Way

In a nursery of twinkling light,
Cosmic babies giggle with delight.
They wriggle and crawl on a starry bed,
With dreams of rockets filling their head.

Galactic lullabies softly hum,
While asteroid toys go thud and thrum.
In this cradle, joy never departs,
As spacemen charm with their wiggly arts.

Comets playing peek-a-boo,
With stardust sprinkled like playful dew.
And when the night grows quiet and deep,
They dream of adventures, then drift to sleep.

With every tick of a cosmic clock,
Giggles burst like a comet's shock.
In this cradle where laughter sways,
Joyfully swirling through the Milky Way!

Stars as Pillows

Fluffy clouds, oh soft delight,
Stars as pillows in the night.
Snuggled tight in cosmic fluff,
Galactic dreams are really tough!

Sleepy suns take a gentle sway,
Whispering tales of fiery ways.
While sparkly twinkles begin to play,
In this slumber, we drift away.

Shooting stars are bedtime snacks,
Nibbling on light's radiant tracks.
As we giggle through midnight scenes,
In dreamland, we conquer worlds unseen.

So when you lay your weary head,
Know laughter follows where you tread.
On celestial pillows, dreams take flight,
With every star, a laugh ignites!

Home of the Midnight Whispers

In a nook where shadows speak,
Laughter plays hide and seek.
Cats dress up in cosmic hats,
While mice debate with cheeky chats.

Echoes of a midnight clown,
Juggling dreams, he never frowns.
Socks fall in a stellar race,
Winners paint the moon with grace.

Whispers drift on comet tails,
Tickling the tips of happy trails.
Got a spaceship made of cheese?
Who's ready for a cosmic tease?

Underneath the funny lights,
Silly dances set the nights.
Joy unfolds in twinkling sparks,
As giggles echo through the dark.

Interstellar Embrace of Love

Two star-crossed marshmallows hug,
Dancing on a comet's rug.
They trip over stardust giggles,
Curling up in cosmic wiggles.

With every twinkle, hearts collide,
In a spaceship as their guide.
Moonbeams turn to love's sweet brew,
Sipping constellations, just a few.

Asteroid pies served at a feast,
Love letters penned by quirky beasts.
Space cows moo in charming tunes,
While fireworks star-dance with the moons.

In this universe of fun,
Embraces spark like an old run.
Together they'll drift through the lore,
Cosmic giggles forevermore.

Lyrical Nights in a Celestial Retreat

When the sky sings a lullaby,
Floats a chicken, oh so spry.
Quacking notes in a cosmic key,
Lyrical whims set the night free.

Shooting stars, a comet's race,
Bouncing beans, a starlit chase.
The moon strums its golden guitar,
While sunbeams dance near a candy jar.

In the quiet, giggles abound,
Where quirky critters swirl around.
Dancing shadows on the floor,
Swaying rhythm, can't ignore.

Riddles whispered in the dark,
Each riddle blooms like a spark.
Celestial tunes invite us near,
To laugh and play, our hearts sincere.

Comforting Shadows of the Cosmos

In the cozy dark, dreams roam,
Cuddly creatures find their home.
A sleeping bear snores in delight,
While owls giggle at the sight.

Moonlit marbles roll and play,
Dancing shadows at the bay.
An octopus in pajamas, so bright,
Serves popcorn under starry light.

Comet trails spin tales so sweet,
Tickling toes and twirling feet.
Imagine socks with polka dots,
And bear hugs in the wormy knots.

Echoes dance through the velvet skies,
As twilight gives us goofy sighs.
In this realm where laughter thrives,
Cosmic jesters pull all our lives.

The Cradle of Night Secrets

In shadows where whispers creep,
The raccoons hold their nightly meet.
With glowing eyes and cheeky grins,
They plot to sneak the human's bins.

The owls hoot with laughter loud,
As squirrels dance beneath the cloud.
While fireflies play hide and seek,
The night is lively, cheeky, and bleak.

Beneath the moon's mischievous grin,
The critters laugh, it's hard to win.
A cat leaps high, a flash of fur,
But then it's gone—just a blur!

With each twinkling light that plays,
The night unveils its funny ways.
In this chaos, joy does swell,
Where secrets dance, and laughter dwells.

Hearths Ignited by Celestial Passions

Gather 'round, the stars ignite,
With tales of love and silly fright.
The moon blushes in its glow,
As lovebirds flap and put on a show.

The comet streaks, a fiery wink,
While dogs just bark and cats just think.
In dreams, the fireplace roars,
Tales of romance behind closed doors.

Mismatched socks and clumsy tries,
To woo a heart beneath the skies.
They slip, they slide, oh what a scene,
As hearts aflame spark giggles between.

With laughter echoing through the night,
Let's toast to love and its delight.
May every ember's crackle tell,
Of goofy romances that do well.

Starlit Pathways of Memory

Take a stroll where sparkles gleam,
Each twinkle tells a silly dream.
We tripped on paths of laughter bright,
Where memories dance, a pure delight.

With friends who snort at every joke,
The stars above, they gently poke.
Each footstep echoes tales untold,
Of goofy moments, daring and bold.

We stop to chase a shooting star,
But trip on shoes that wander far.
The cosmos laughs, a wink so wide,
At all the joyful flubs we bide.

As laughter ripples through the night,
Each memory glows, a silly sight.
In starlit dreams where we once ran,
The funny times forever span.

Night's Gentle Embrace

As twilight falls with a playful sigh,
The frogs begin their night-time cry.
With soft croaks, they sing their song,
While stars above just hum along.

The wind whispers secrets with a grin,
As shadows dance, let the fun begin.
A raccoon steals a picnic snack,
And trips on toes, then hops right back!

Cats in the garden, doing their thing,
With paws that swish, oh what a fling!
They pounce on shadows with glorious flair,
While humans giggle, unaware of their dare.

In this embrace of tales untold,
Where night unfolds with joys bold.
A symphony of laughter, wild and free,
In gentle arms of night, we see.

Hushed Conversations in Starlit Dwellings

Whispers float like fireflies,
Secrets shared with twinkling eyes,
Jokes about the moon's latest phase,
Laughter echoes through the night maze.

A cat dreams of catching a star,
While folks argue where they will park the car,
Chairs creak beneath the cosmos' weight,
As we toast to dreams that can wait.

Candy wrappers dance in the breeze,
Roofs play host to ants and bees,
Each one's tale is a goofy hit,
Mixed up socks hide where they sit.

Just don't wake the sleeping owl,
Or he'll tell jokes that make you howl,
Underneath this mystical glow,
Life's a circus, but we love the show.

Souls Connected by Nightfall

Giggling shadows creep up the walls,
As someone slips and nearly falls,
Stars are jealous of our fun,
They twinkle harder, one by one.

A raccoon rummages near the light,
Critiques our picnic in the night,
Banging tables up and down,
While kids wear smiles instead of frowns.

Whipped cream fights break out with glee,
Slinging blobs becomes the key,
In this dreamy play of fate,
Messy hands don't discriminate.

Nighttime mischief knows no bounds,
As we spin tales with silly sounds,
Each laugh echoes in the dark,
Our spirits light up like a spark.

A Journey through the Celestial Garden

Bubbles floating to galaxies bright,
Brought a curious, giggling sprite,
Chasing dreams in moonlit glades,
While ice cream melts in radiant shades.

We weave through flowers that giggle too,
Joking why the stars missed their cue,
With seeds that chatter, dressed up in hues,
Mixing stardust with evening's blues.

Oh, look—there's a comet that sneezed!
Sending wishes to those who asked, pleased!
Tickled pink by a celestial prank,
Space whispers secrets from the flank.

In this garden of cosmic surprise,
Plum pie secrets and autumn skies,
Frolic on paths where stars sway,
Together we dream the night away.

Dancing with Shooting Stars

With toes tapping on the bright green grass,
We twirl beneath space's vast glass,
Shooting stars join in the spree,
Flipping and flapping, oh what glee!

The moon plays DJ, spinning tunes,
While crickets chirp funky cartoons,
Each step is a wobble, a bounce, a leap,
As laughter rings through the mountains deep.

Cloud-whispers tell of future days,
When we'll spin tales in silly ways,
Chasing stardust just like we want,
Silly dances with a cosmic flaunt.

Even constellations join the fun,
Forming figures that come undone,
Underneath this joyous trance,
Life's a grand and goofy dance.

An Oasis of Night

In a yard full of crickets' song,
We gather, munching on snacks all night long.
With lemonade mustaches, we laugh out loud,
As fireflies dance, making us proud.

A blanket's fortress, a snack attack,
Who knew stargazing could lead to this? A whack!
With marshmallows flying through the air,
We're the best circus, without a care.

Telling ghost stories that make us squeal,
Imagining aliens who steal our meal.
Under a canopy of diamond winks,
We giggle at shadows, pour soda in drinks.

As dawn creeps in, the stars take flight,
Our laughter still echoing into the night.
We pack up this oasis with a smile,
Promising to return in just a little while.

Connecting Hearts among the Andromeda

We painted our dreams on a cosmic page,
Each twinkle and blink, a digital rage.
With Wi-Fi stars and satellite bars,
We connect our hearts, just wish on the stars.

Playing hide and seek with a comet's tail,
We chase 'round planets, our voices a trail.
Laughing at aliens who can't find Wi-Fi,
In this galaxy, we're the link, oh my!

A dance party with Saturn, those rings a delight,
We bump into space where asteroids fight.
Our friendship's a rocket, let's fuel it up,
Navigating the cosmos, with laughter to sup.

The universe spins, but we hold on tight,
Spinning tales of love in the moon's soft light.
With each starburst laughter and sighs so grand,
We twinkle together, hand in hand.

When the Sky Becomes Our Ceiling

The roof's on vacation, it flew to the moon,
We're lounging below, in our silly festoon.
With a rooftop of clouds, we're flipping some pies,
Underneath this vast dome, we're kings and we're wise.

The stars are our lanterns, shining so bright,
As we tell each other ghost stories of fright.
With each spooky tale, the owls hoot back,
And laughter erupts, like a fresh soda attack.

Pickle jar rockets, we launch to the night,
Not sure where they land, it's quite a delight.
Under a sky where the sun shouldn't be,
We wonder aloud, "What's that up in the tree?"

There's no four walls to keep us confined,
Our imaginations run, brightly aligned.
When the sky is our ceiling, there's room to play,
We'll stay here forever, let's not go away!

Timeless Trysts Beneath Galaxies

Two squirrels debate at the base of a tree,
Gathering nuts, plotting a wild jubilee.
While we study the dance of each twinkling star,
Who knew friendship flourished just this bizarre?

Our picnic's a feast fit for kings of the sky,
With peanut butter sandwiches, oh me, oh my!
As laughter erupts, the raccoons all cheer,
Timeless moments, perfectly sincere.

Those meteors zooming, a celestial race,
We cheer them along, grant them a space.
"Make a wish!" we shout as they fall from afar,
Each one a promise, our own shooting star.

Under the brilliance where wild dreams reside,
When squirrels roll their eyes, there's nowhere to hide.
Timeless, we linger, our hearts full of glee,
Beneath the magic, just you, stars, and me.

www.ingramcontent.com/pod-product-compliance
Lightning Source LLC
Chambersburg PA
CBHW062112280426
43661CB00086B/497